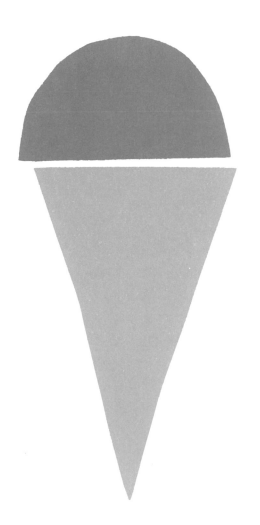

First Chronicle Books edition published in 2006.

Book design by Paul Rand.
Manufactured in China.

Library of Congress Cataloging-in-Publication Data
Rand, Ann.
Sparkle and spin : a book about words / by Ann & Paul Rand.
—1st Chronicle Books ed.
p. cm.
Summary: Lyrical text explores what words are and how they are used,
highlighting such characteristics as that some words sound like what they mean,
some make one feel a certain way, some are spoken softly, and some are shouted.
ISBN 13: 978-0-8118-5003-2 / ISBN 10: 0-8118-5003-X
[1. English language—Etymology—Fiction. 2. Communication—Fiction.]
I. Rand, Paul, 1914- II. Title.
PZ7.R152Sp 2006
[E]—dc22
2004023260

Distributed in Canada by Raincoast Books
9050 Shaughnessy Street, Vancouver, British Columbia V6P 6E5

10 9 8 7 6 5 4 3 2

Chronicle Books LLC
680 Second Street, San Francisco, California 94107

www.chroniclekids.com

Sparkle

and

Spin

A book about words
by Ann & Paul Rand

chronicle books · san francisco

What are words?
Words are how what you think inside
comes out
and how to remember what you might
forget about.

A word is a thing
you heard or saw
or can even draw a
picture of.
Words are the names of objects
like book and doll and chair
or of animals
like bird and dog and bear.

AB
CD
EF
GH
IJ
KL
MN
OP
QR
ST
UV
WX
YZ

Words are the names of people
you like:
Sally and Mary,
Thomas and Harry.
Words tell how you feel:
fine and dandy
and I like candy.

They also say what you can do:
jump and run
and have a lot of fun.
Words can ask for what you want:
Where are my shoes?
Or bring you news
from the wide world over.

New York
NESDAY, JANUAR
Special to The New York T
NORTHAMPTON, Ma
29—The President of
College questioned to
adequacy of the object
of the College Entrance
nation Board as a mean
dicting success in colle
Dr. Benjamin F. Wrig
enth annual report as
of the college for won
with the problem of
an entering class of slig
600 from more than 2,
cants, all of whom take
lege Board examinatio
These examinations
tests that can be gr
chanically, he said, ra
vith questions of the

N

Words are "Yes I will"
and "No I won't,"
but they are polite too
like please and thank you.

TINTINNABU

Some words are as big
as tintinnabulate,
while a word like <u>a</u>,
as you can see,
is just as small
as a baby bumblebee.

Words can say
how hot the sun has got,
or tell
how pretty a seashell is.

And surely you've found
words sometimes sound
exactly like what they're
supposed to be.
There's toot toot!
whee! and whoa!
And when you hear about
the rumbling rolling roar
of thunder,
you never have to wonder
what it is.

Some words are gay and bright
and full of light
like tinsel and silver
and sparkle and spin,
while lurk and murk
or moan and groan
are just as dark as night.

A word is something you shout,
bang! or boo!
when you jump out
from behind a chair,
or something to whisper softly
as the little breeze
that says "hush hush"
as it rustles the leaves.
A word can warn that
someone's sick
or bring somebody running quick!

Sometimes one word sounds
the same as another
like hair and hare
or pair and pear.

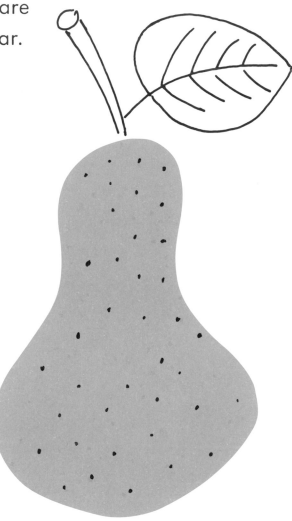

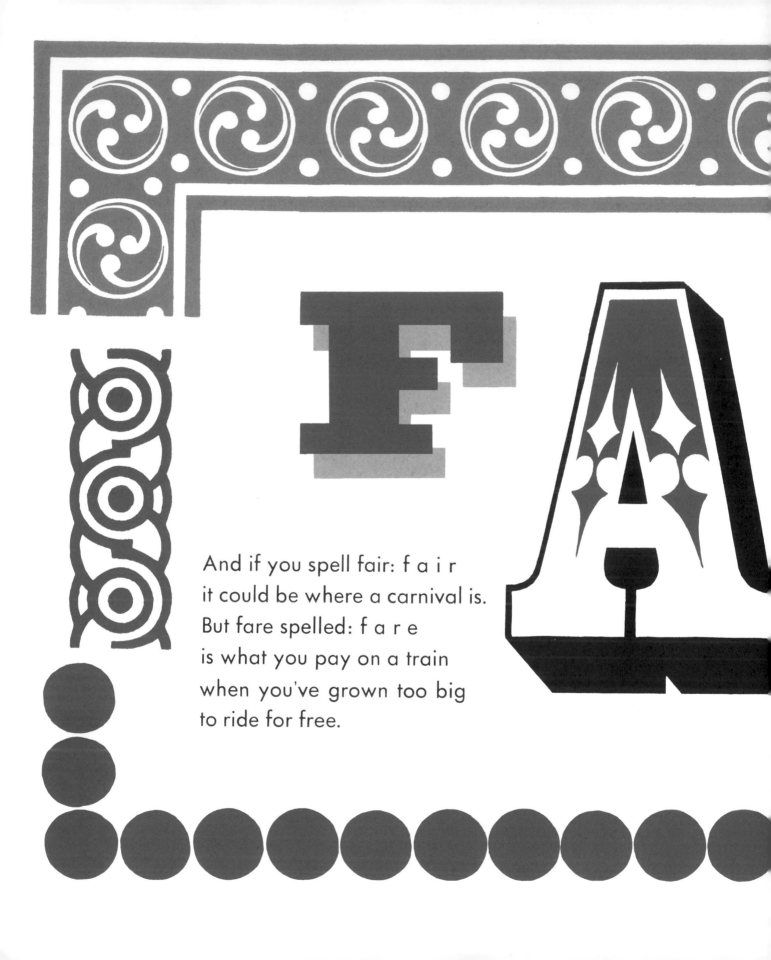

And if you spell fair: f a i r
it could be where a carnival is.
But fare spelled: f a r e
is what you pay on a train
when you've grown too big
to ride for free.

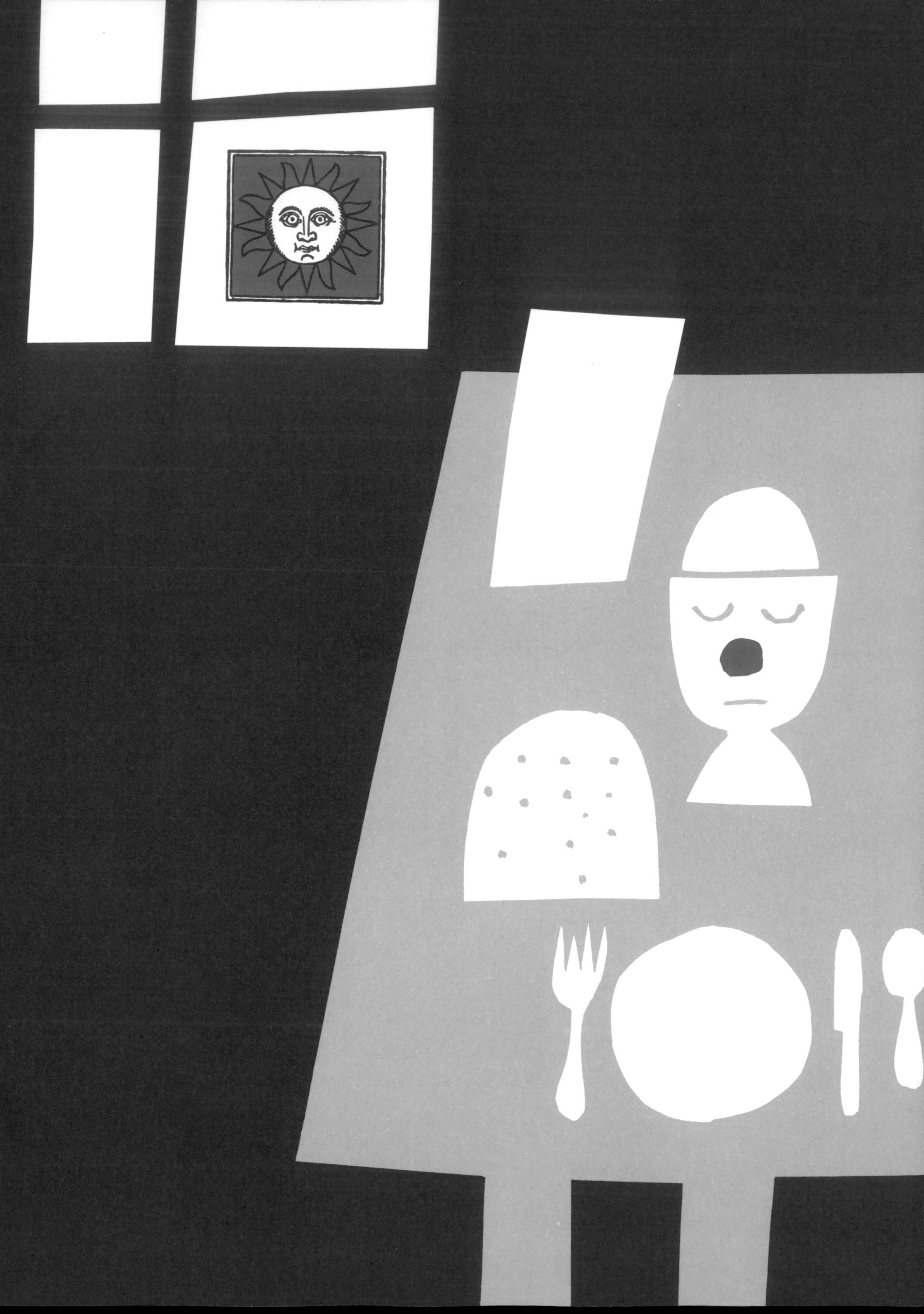

Words can say,
wake up, wake up!
The day is fine,
the sun will shine.

Words can sing a song
or say "good night, Mother."

This is what words are for.
All these and many more
teach us how
to talk to one another.

The End